This is a journey of displaced identity—an exile, a dystopia—constantly in search of a home that is nowhere to be found, except on the landscape of language where reality and all its known and unknown possibilities dwell as cohabitants. They exist in a constant flux of love-hate and love-again relationships, exactly in the way human life flows and confronts death and forgetting.

This collection is a whirlwind of conversations. It is a memoir, sort of love letters, and also an ongoing dialogue between the man and his times.

Our Nights were born
in the Streets

Sarbajit Sarkar

HAWAKAL

HAWAKAL

Published by Hawakal Publishers
185 Kali Temple Road, Nimta, Kolkata 700049
India

Email info@hawakal.com
Website www.hawakal.com

First edition August, 2019

Copyright © Mridula Sarkar 2019

Cover photograph: Canva
Cover design: Bitan Chakraborty

ISBN: 978-93-87883-77-2

Price: INR 250 | USD 7.99

for
my mother

CONTENTS

SORT OF LOVE POEMS

SPEAK, MEMORY

After Vladimir Nabokov's autobiographical memoir.

Reading

I dream you'll come back again
and lie down like a lost fragrance
in a bed of yellow leaves. If you come
I think I'll pick up the forgotten books.

The books too dream you'll return someday.
They belong to a city that speaks through them.

The city nudges the books when they slumber.
It holds them together.
And fills them with silent stillness of its streets,
by-lanes, stone chips and shops and bazaars
and swarm of men and darkness and lights
and shadows..all stoned beneath a sprawling
umbrella of loneliness.
This is the way books come back to life
and patiently wait to welcome you, hoping
you'll be back soon.

They are afraid that you might leave again.
So, they plot to suck you in.
They whisper to tell you: reading is a journey,
never to end.

A Mark

It's good to leave a mark,
you told me
even if it remains nameless,
like falling leaves;
drifting,
clasping emptiness...
In acceptance,
in rejection,
or in forgetting.

It's the genius of roving nails
that walk with my age every day.
I don't talk of love anymore.
Color of sunshine is a strange grasshopper;
it keeps moving from shadows to light
to shadows again, repeating itself
so that I don't talk about love anymore.

Behind the dark clouds, you come
like lightning flashes
to see me at times.
I don't talk of love anymore.

I stay silent.
May be, in silence,
I speak of love once again.

Breath of those dead stars

Do you remember
You held me
close to your breast
so that, the breathing
of those distant stars
could embrace you too
through the night, once again?

I was surprised.
Am I the breathing of those
dead stars!
Can I be the breath
of the silent stars
million light-years away
to bring you their warmth tonight?

To this, you cuddled
more, to close down
on my lips.

So then, that's how, do death
when it gets so close
becomes the warmth
of our lives?

Face

I was lost.
I wished to be lost.
That's the reason
I chose all the faces.

To them, who were shocked to see
my anger, my hatred,
 my disgust, my spite and my violence,
I wish to tell that
I also was scared.
To the bones.

I too wished to see myself.
Dreamed to be a river,
for whom, memories of her body
was nothing but the shadows
of a million faces, forever drifting away.

Between my unfolded praying hands
I caressed those lovely faces
and asked each of them,
Teach me how to swim;
teach me, how to swim.

Journal

This is my life.
A little insane, a little wasted
mostly thrown away, withered, and dumped.

Frail glow of a shadowy dusk
spread it's wings over the tramway rails

Love adorned me in its simplest forms
till I strangled it with my own hands

In our old ancestral house
the termites, the rats, and the roots of an
ancient banyan tree
feverishly search for their soul

It seems, all things that I owned
awaits the sinking touch
of my own killing hands

And now everything is happening
in the desperate name of love.
Sadly, you don't ask me why?

What You can Expect from a Poet

Don't expect calm if you have loved a poet,
let his slow burn emit a soft glow,
warm yourself with his brief candle's light,
don't be afraid when his wildfire engulfs dark
forests.

He tells you,
If the stars destroy me in their wrath
kiss me as in a prayer and
if a haunted wind cry out over the railway tracks
hold your silent gush, beloved, and get back to your
solitude.

He says,
paths in the woods are burning
and that fire on bird-wings is a fugitive;
a cold blaze in eternal flames;
you can watch it burn,
from afar.

Lost Love

Raskolnikov
I think the name is enough
to charter a path between
agony and punishment.

But redemption is a nowhere city.

My address belongs to the state register
Do I have those plastic cards?
Do I have that plastic card that codes
my name, address, whereabouts,
proofs that sustain we are citizens?

But halfway they are lost.
Because our love knows no bound
and it couples with ecstasy
to baffle the plastic cards.

And we say,
I come...You come..I come... You come...
This way, only-way
we can keep our citadel
unfound by them.

Sita

Dear girl, don't trust a man who comes
with his begging bowl.
Don't ponder:
is it love, or money, is it for your body, or is it
for a bowl of rice, it could be for your kindness or your
forgiveness even:
forget it, don't ascertain
it's no point what he is asking for.
Just don't trust him anyways.

Be careful, girl
you may cross the circle if you so wish
but check out before you do
see if he is carrying a bowl, check if it's begging
do check if he demands your wholeness
before giving anything to you.

And if you see
he is promising everything
when he asks for your hand
you can be sure his bowl is already full
with the chameleon lust of *Ravana*.

In that case you have nothing else to give
except to lose yourself, forever.

A Roadside Front-door

It looks so similar
and yet so distant
as if something
fragile in memory.

Even the shadows,
that the streetlights portray,
remind me of you.

Home
Calcutta
1982

A midnight with broken poles
uprooted trees, lost bird-nests
clasping together,
were lying on the ground
trying to save a birth.

Flood on street, knee-deep.
I am coming back home
but darkness signs me off.

Years pass.
I notice the pavement tiles have changed.
And the stroller has changed too.

Getway to Reality

Do you shag?
They asked me on board
to my first job.
I was twenty-one.
Year 1983.
No Shopping Malls
and twelve variety of toothpastes then.
Condom – a rubber cloth for family planning.

I didn't know what they meant
but still I nodded.

Yes! Something whispered in my head;
Yes is the key to deal power-brokers.

Hell knows I needed that job.
My mother had sad eyes
 holding on to her dreams.

Knowing or unknowing
didn't make sense to me.
They are like canned drinks,

energy-shooters, packed well
they make-beliefs.

I believe
Despair is the key to satisfy hunger.

That's the moment I entered you: Reality.
And poetry started following me: like a sleuth.
Destined, not to die.

For the Gift I Received

I ask you to hold my hand and take me
to some other time. I thought that-time
will be: You.
I see yellow leaves slowly coming down
on roads pummeled with shadows and light.
Only once, I wish to see my birth:
to see how the earth smiled the day I was born
and to hear that first cry I blew.

What else I could offer you for this gift received,
Mother Earth?

Neighbors

She spent the morning drying washed clothes
my neighbor, a widow, I call her aunt,
How are you aunty? I asked
I'm fine, she said, *hope you're fine too.*

Half a life we spend trusting these few words.
The other half knotted with targets, archers and ennui.

Sometimes the moon comes closer
dressed in orange and yellow, with little spots of grey,
as if in mourning, stands alone
on our terrace, and
on our neighbor's terrace too.

Life surpasses us.

Pilgrims

Certainly someday
they will find out this book
while walking
through the riddled roads of
blood and dreams.

Forlorn, desolate
they will sit for a while
to have their crumbs of
bread and wine
and will think that,

Only when a heart breaks
it learns to love.
Who am I, without exile?

They will pick up the book,
those sulking travelers,
as they rise to walk
on the roads of
that pilgrim city
sleeping inside them.

GAMING CONSOLE

Our Nights were Born in the Streets

To open the bedroom door in the middle of night:
that's art.
To open it in a way that the woman asleep in bed
won't even hear the faint screech, no sounds to
follow through, and like the hell-door about to
open, or suddenly like a slit opening in a dying
man's throat, the door opens, a resounding screech
again, the door scratches its frame..nothing more
is needed: to become art.

It tempts you to be swift like a tiger, sly-mover
like a fox, it goads you to bear a killer's eyes that
cling to the wintry days of his nerves. Or, do you
need something more? Something like the apathy
of a man leaving home eight years before.

Or it could be a thousand years more, when he
was drawn to the secret serenade of nights, left
the luxury of his sleeping wife, left home,
indifferent, to savor the soliloquy of stygian
nocturnes. That's what all art is calling for.

Night: 1947

When night speaks, listen.
She travelled through the stories of births and
deaths,
of wars, tales told by pall bearers,
of roses and lovers, she knows the cities and
their hydrants,
listen to her;
between deaths and births
between the pall bearers and the assassins
between lovers and withering roses
where a city is hiding itself, there
night is telling its tale,
to her, you listen.

Night: 2018

What can words tell you?
A wave is sleeping in another wave.
And there are waves: ad infinitum.
What will the words tell you!

Night: 1947

Behind the shadows
someone is talking.
Someone deported, someone who lost
a home.
He could be somewhat loony
except, when he writes
those unnamed pains
that are fluid and dark.

And they slowly rise through his nerves.

Night: 2018

I see a strange moon over the kid's school
pointing a heedless gun
at blind men across the town;
someone in the distance is waving a hand
to say a last goodbye,
I can smell their body odor
quietly creeping inside books
piled in libraries of ancient cities
tonight.

Night: 1947

Bazaars and crossroads are born surrounding
us.Frontiers are drawn against barbed wires.
Bloodsheds in streets happen. Ripper and the riot
police vibrate together. Typefaces grow as
garbages. Letters, alphabets, words, become
germicides of pure intellect. They come without
truth, without any blood dripping inside them.

I seek the unwritten addresses behind every
word
that the words themselves forgot to write.

Night: 2018

I could never come back.
Never returned from the landscape
of one lonely planet to another.
Of course this is the only one
I ever had.
Its earthy water held me tight.
Its ancient colonies and their conquests

were growing inside my head;
I carried a fire and a storm
in my heart, and in this planet of
water and fire and air
I keep looking for myself.
I am looking for the alphabets
that can write down my dialogue
with this planet, it's as lost as I am.

Night: 1947

Birds and twilight know the path to every sunset
birds like humans watch their faces in drifting water
somebody from past years call them back
someone from tomorrow calls them forth
birds and twilights throughout their life
feed on seeds scattered in the great unknown.

Night: 2018

I have multiple mirrors inside my veins
where I look for your fragmented face
sliced memories, torn pages of a family album.
Silence of broken homes, accompanies me
while I search .
I can hear our voices, faded to an extent,
but still echoing in the room. They still hold
the sharp edges of a razor. I hear them
sinking deep in the void.
However I can't fathom the depth they go.
I presume they will reach the place
where an unborn child, still in sleep, is listening
to our conversation.
But all these, didn't it happen long ago,
once upon a time?

Night: 1947
I couldn't see death. I had hopes. Everybody had.
We celebrated that midnight.
Like children we celebrated.
Out in the streets, on roads, we didn't hear the sound
of the wheels of slow tram-cars coming behind us.
Slow deaths are less painful, aren't they?

Night: 2018
Something more happened that night.
I can see men crossing rivers.
Men, women, children.
Crossing dark waters and plains. I hear gunshots and
sudden cries, screams, tearing down the all pervading
lull of a dead night.
I see a man trying to kiss the wings of a butterfly.
I think
he was dreaming. We think they were dreaming.
Like all nations do.
I think the man himself thought he was dreaming.
Why else he would be signing
a suicide note on that night?

Night: 1947
I am feeling tired. Can I go and sleep?
I lived in my hope. So you do.
Do questions take us anywhere?
Ain't there big hands that deal the cards
and pull the strings?
Night: 2018
I wake up in a world brimming with tales.
Tales to remember. Tales not to forget.

I wake up in a city where the butchers
ignore the last cries of birds. It's a city of cages.
I see the butcher enjoying a song on radio
as he cuts her throat. What a pleasure, he thinks!
I see a fluid moonlight entering people's hearts.
Soft dull yellow in color. It kicks people's sleeping
and wondering souls at night, I don't know why!
I sit beside you to listen to your stories.
I thought, it will not end.
It should never end.

Night: 1947
I will tell you a story. It's a story of now.
If you follow the nurse coming out of the hospital
you get to a balcony. Stand there facing her. Ask her
why she is having dreams of a rainy day
and a windy day?
Why is she dreaming of grasslands, broken basins,
closed doors, and barbed wires? Why a pistol keeps
coming back in her dreams?
Then give your hand to her. Let her hold it, silently.
Let moments pass.

Night: 2018
I know people who keep their windows open
in the middle of the night: to face death.
I know how they yearn to listen to stories that life tells.

Night: 1947
I will speak. And I will wait to hear your tales.
Through the nights our stories will move.
A day, like the drunk, or an addict, is nearing its end.
I will sit beside that day to say something,

but what should I say...what...?

Night: 2018

This is the last conversation we have.
It sounds like wailing of a wounded bird, or
like a prisoner marking on the wall
of his solitary cell
one..two..three...

Shooting Targets

I think this century too will die soon.
If you can, try remember its stories of weed-fed deaths.
Remember how their words lived.
Memory: the shooting target for men with guns.

A road used to call by my name.
Did you ever want to know which one?
I dream of going back to that place.
Every time. Everywhere.

But there are dead names that block my path:
Surjo, Kobita, Peto, Shibe, Aarshad

A lie, a lie, a lie, a lie
all alike is a lie; but that's what they preach in TV
to claim that dead men are dead men. Without name
without face, without a sky.

But then again dead names come and block my path
humming their simple lullaby, that says remember,
Memory is the shooting target for all men with guns.

In My Century

It's easy
in our century
to write wounded stories
of being defeated

be a lamp instead
be a flame, glow

watch that naked light
walking through landscapes
in an unfettered flow

A Hot Day

Okay, so it's two at noon.
I draw one from the cigarette pack
puff it twice, do not inhale
but let the smoke go out
and face the air marshal fan
speeding overhead.

In TV they are showing a heated debate
on rape accused of Unnao,
hot spit surges forth
from mouths of dueling speakers
 as my remote gets hotter
 since I'm holding it too long,
so hot that the spectacle on screen,
oblivious to my cigarette smoke,
outcasts and overshadows
the salt-soaked tear of the rape victim
battling for her life
in some obscure hospital bed.

The day will remain to be hot
as long as they depend
on binary to solve everything

even for something as cold as rape.

Stories about Killings

Rainclouds that hover over Bijon Setu
translate my desperate dreams, and
teach me to read your moments of scarred breath.

Don't blame the day if the sky becomes a manuscript
that it gnaws your heart, and the ancient moss
that has grown there, get entangled and
bleed. Be careful; don't touch them with your tongue.

You think the tales gone old to tell anymore?
Point is: we have nowhere to go. So we repeat.

And killings happen easily, almost every day
and nobody knows why,
at dawn a breeze blows over terraces
and starts writing the first chapters.

What if the wind could hear the stories once told?

Probably we could get our stories renewed then.

Storyline

You were turning the pages
and suddenly stopped at one point;
what was the page number,
do you remember?
you were unable to move beyond

now you have come to me asking
what was there in your story?

Your story: Story of your life
I wonder why you come to me
to know what was thereafter.

you are shuttling between one address
and another, shifting from moment
to moment, running through galaxies
of information, knowledge, history
just to know, what is written in
your story, beyond this point, and
at the end of it.

Bewakuf! Look at yourself
listen to your heart, ask him

what does he want
what does he wish to be

And this is what I can tell you
believe in your desires and dreams

read yourself, that's only what is true.

Few Things I know about Mass Killing

A cowbell rings in distraught
yelling men can be heard
but only from a distance,
on TV screens. Nowhere else.

Under a mango tree they rope him
I can hear the lashes that seem
like snakes hissing;
no one can see the venom
that flows mid-air.

There must be hundreds like that
all buried untraced.

Next month it rains
mud covers up the field
people sow seeds,
nothing is visible anymore.

Villagers at the end of the year
will only see the butterflies

flirting with the mustard flowers
as they spread their wings to fly.

A flight is a flight is a flight.
Lynching is only a bad memory.

Everything's cool!
Except when the vultures come back
and fly in circles above the mustard field

drawn by stink
to dig up the dead
from memories.

The Room in Hotel Anandalok

I slept like a river the entire day
and woke up at night to speak.
I saw how the day was getting on its edge.
Seized by its overflowing bazaars
hubris, dumb crowds, and rambling coins.

Probably, the silence of this hotel room
should be blamed that I am awake tonight.
I think the room knows that all earthly stories
are born from its womb. A womb that can
only belong to a roadside hotel:
secret, lonesome, aloof, and solitary.

It knows everything. Death of a salesman,
stories of their love lives and sins. How they
deal with customers and destiny, how they win
they cheat, how they sail in defeat, everything
the room knows. It knows that
market is the father to every miracle on this earth.
And bazaars are strange things. Even if a million
death hold their tongue and chokes their throat
they will not stop howling.

Tonight, the room whispers to me what it never
disclosed so far. That, in the lonely hours of night
it is writing a novel: for eternity.
A novel about, killings, gallows,
borders, darkness, defeats,
kisses and hopes, and ancient banyan trees.

So I stay awake, tonight, and listen
to its myriad voice, the witch-voice that calls
the past to confront the present
and seeds the present to dream their tomorrows
and says,
Let the veins that carry my blood
get soaked in an afternoon-light
and wake up in their dreams
to see a tomorrow of hope, approaching them.

A Surreal Poem

As they went further down, deeper, and as they traveled wide, the words, moved into other towns and cities. They were like water: formed and unformed, often in splashes and sometimes in serenity. They were brought up by lust and also by indifference. They were reminding us that we must settle down beside a river or a lake. We are the ones to carry the religion of water, they said. The beasts came at night to quench their thirst. Stream of silent waves were happy to see them. Stars were glowing bright. Our Word watched everything. And finally he told her, *don't put on the light. Not now. Let the world know that we are happy together.* We have enough grains, and raindrops, and memories, and tears, and laughter, with us, to stay alive, till death.

SORT OF LOVE POEMS

Radha Says
(for Reetika Vazirani)

Why did you die?
I kept looking at her gray photograph.
She kept smiling.
Why did you have to die? I asked her again,
her smile was gleaming.
See the eyes, see the eyes, and inside those
irises the two white spots! It's the light
I could not contain. I slashed the wrist to see
how crimson appealed, Radha said.

A Sea in You

I have been trying to change myself
for many years now.

If I could grab my collar
and drag myself to the sea
to look at the horizon it draws,
and suppose I said,
if you want to give,
give it all like the sea,

my life could have been
different then.

Much less like somebody else
but more like what I could be.

Remembering Vincent

A hundred and fifty-year-old night: you took the first step to revisit its dark hours. No one was inside the room where darkness formed a mist. You saw the table at the centre. On top of it you sensed a candle that stood on a white china plate. As you lit a match a night bird flew through the window. You shuddered. Your eyes had adapted to the darkness now. You lit a second matchstick to find the trembling shadow of your finger on the opposite wall. A blue flame was rising in the dark. It quivered in orange and yellow aura. It's the color that crossed the borders of your canvases. You stretched your left hand and put your palm over the flame, but it shirked, wiggled and shrank only to hit back with all its strength. It became a snake to sting your flesh. You feel the heat where it hurts. The flame lashes its tongue against it. You hold your left hand tight over the flame. It shouldn't escape. You cannot escape. The skin burns. You don't feel it. Skin has lost its senses. The candle is melting. The wax is coming down in drops. The burnt odor circles inside the room.

They are the same whirling circles that travel in your cypress-nights. The flame is now touching the flesh.

Someone nails down two words in my head. Despair and Desire. Probably it will be easier for me now to say: I love you, Vincent.

Sparrows on the Wall

Three sparrows sit on a broken wall.
In perfect harmony.
Equally distanced from each other.

I imagine, will they sing?
Broken wall with peeling color is waiting.
I worry, will it crash tomorrow?
Or, is it day-after?

Three sparrows sit still
and keep moving their heads.
To fly? Or to sing? I wonder.
Will it crumble before they do?

I keep wondering with something like hope.

Arrested Soul

As they went further down, deeper, and they travelled wide, in other towns and cities, the words, like water, formed and unformed, in splashes and in serenity, in lust and yet in distancing, reminding us every time, that it's true we live beside some lake, or may be a brook, where a rain suddenly cajoles its waterbody, and the beasts come at night to quench their thirst, and then evening prods my soul, as I tell her, do not put on the light, not now, let the words know we are happy together, tonight:

I say our storerooms are full
with raindrops and nocturne, more water, and
leftovers,
memories are aging wounds
for us, for animals, staying afloat and
embedded until death.

Morning Light
(Remebering Mahmoud Darwish in exile)

Remnants of the endless sky stay inside us.
They have taken the shape of clouds,
holding the water our cries bear.

All our memories are seized and shut.

They remind me today how joyous
and gleaming this morning is.
We are guests of the eternal dawn.

Rain Falling on Leaves

I listen to the *panwala* in this land of torrid heat.
He tells me stories of men and women
in love and in grief, of dragonflies,
weaving in the sun.
They are mundane stories mostly, of their life,
and I tell him, *It's too hot to survive in this place,*
and he points his finger up to the sky and says,
It's His grace!
Remember that happiness comes from Him as well.

Not a single cloud anywhere to be seen,
no rain falls, no river anywhere near this land
and still the man speaks raindrops, and
tell me stories of winding *purvaiyan...*
I wonder how he tells!

Is there a stream softly flowing somewhere
beneath this charred earth?

Writing

Writing is more like melted soaps.
They sleep with letters from groggy billboards
in a bed of white foam.
Their withered alphabets conceal the tears,
and masked prologues of people living inside.
You can see the nail marks of those people
who slashed their flesh from beneath.
People sculpt them like a child's
first feel for words: heavy, dark and scribbled.
Soon the teardrops, like muddy water in puddles,
sticky and mugging, rob the glyphs from people's
fingers and hold them to their hearts.
Writing outlives the lives of people in pain.

Lyric

A ruin—plundered more with your silence...
Songs of sullen stones fetch the nights.
You call them the nightly blues.
Beasts, screaming from eternity,
come and drink the blues.
And you ask them,
why they didn't quit the twilight lament.
Why did they allow it to approach the horizon?

This afternoon, this rain-washed sundown
is no zone to escape to immortality!

As in a Sea, As in the City

I wished nothing, even when
 you all retorted with a straight No,
I never said, *I want.*
When rain lashes the earth a fragrance is born,
I call it *maya.*

Men do all things, they go shopping, have
haircuts,
get into brawl, scale fishes, stand as candidates
in elections, read newspapers,
they sink lips into lips and kiss hard
and desperately tries to forget everything,
men tangle their tongues to row the boats,
they never know when a sea sleeps.

One who says, *I want nothing,*
and gives back *everything,*
in the dark, in secret, in its largesse
it lures us, to seek dangerously
as in a sea, the same in a city.

Travelling Chords

I travelled long,
let me sit now
and drink some water
and let me feel
the religion that aqua holds.

It's like a simple sentence
walking through
mountains, forests and seas
beyond days, many days
to reach places and times
to talk to weary hearts

it's the only religion that
words and water holds.

Rain

"Give me" and
"Take me."
Between the two speeches
today, midway
over the boulevard
rain came.

The shopkeepers were amazed
to see the rushing crowd
even at nine in the evening.

That these moments are born
like celebrations
is all, that our tired earth
ever desired for itself.

After a long time.
After a long time...

Mystery Story

Mysterious is this tree that offers you its fruit.
Magical is this river that watches you immerse in it.
Miraculous this roadside inn whose loneliness
shakes your body to erupt into a dialogue,
with yourself.
This wind too is overpowering.
It blows to fill up your room.
It stack your books, makes your bed,
and washes your clothes clean.
Aloof is the sky. It gives birth to yearnings and grief.
Alluring is the book that gives you pleasure of reading
while dismantling you into pieces, like a child playing
with building blocks.
How brimming is this starry night!
It sucks your sleepless eyes
and fills you with wanderlust.
It tempts the hunter in you.
These night-walks are enchanting too.
They tell you the love stories
of forbidden fire and ice.
And this woman, is like destiny
who wish to see the end of your love
to keep her dreams alive.

Bodh Gaya

Beside the river *Niranjan*
a moment glanced upon eternity.

The country became a haven.

[Buddha meditated beside the river, *Niranjan,* and achived
Nirvana.]

SARBAJIT SARKAR

Sarbajit is a poet, writer, painter and critic from Kolkata, India. He has seven collections of poetry, and three anthologies of short stories in Bengali. His critical essays on literature and art have been published in several literary journals, like *The Critical Flame*, *The Indian Express*, *Sangbad Pratidin*, *Abahaman*, *4numberplatform*, among other places.

www.ingramcontent.com/pod-product-compliance
Lightning Source LLC
Chambersburg PA
CBHW021145020426
42331CB00005B/897